TRUE
Disciples

Colin Urquhart

Kingdom Faith Resources Ltd.
Roffey Place, Old Crawley Road,
HORSHAM West Sussex, RH12 4RU
Tel: 01293 851543 Fax: 01293 854610
E-mail: resources@kingdomfaith.com
www.kingdomfaith.com

First published in Great Britain in March 2002 by Kingdom Faith

Kingdom Faith Trust is a registered charity (no.278746)

ISBN 1-900409-32-1

Acknowledgements

My thanks to Diane, David and Cliss for all their loving hard work in producing this book; and to the Kingdom Faith team and church for their supportive prayers. They form a wonderful family of faith of which I am privileged to be a part, together with my wife and family. To God be all the glory, the One in whom we put our trust!

CONTENTS

1

THE CALL

Jesus Christ, the Son of God, gathered around Him a group of disciples who spent the three years of His ministry on earth with Him. Before returning to heaven, He gave those men this commission: *"Go and make disciples of all nations." (Matt 28:19)*

This is the work of the church: to make disciples. What does this mean? What, in Jesus' teaching, is a disciple? And how can we make disciples today? Unless we have clear answers to these questions, we could miss God's purpose for our lives!

Jesus called His first disciples early in His ministry. They were not people with worldly influence, neither were they learned or of high social status. They were ordinary fishermen:

As Jesus walked beside the Sea of Galilee, he saw Simon and his brother Andrew casting a net into the lake, for they were fishermen. "Come, follow me," Jesus said, "and I will make you fishers of men". At once they left their nets and followed him. (Mk 1:16-18)

The call of the disciple, then and now, is to follow Jesus. To His disciples Jesus gave ministries, or ways of serving Him. However, we must not confuse their call and their ministry. Their call was to follow Jesus; their ministry to become fishers of men. Their call was to be disciples; their ministries were the ways in which Jesus would use them as His followers.

Their response to the call was immediate and whole-hearted; they left everything to follow Him. Their lives would now be focused around Him, even though at this time they did not know that Jesus was God's Son. Other fishermen, James and his brother, John, were called in a similar fashion to Simon and Andrew. Matthew was called from being a tax-collector, a notorious occupation at the time. To Philip, Jesus simply said: *"Follow me." (Jn 1:43)*

From among all who were drawn to Him, Jesus chose twelve disciples who would enjoy a close relationship with Him, travelling wherever He went, listening to Him teach and witnessing the healings and miracles He performed.

Before selecting these twelve, Jesus spent a whole night praying to His Father. It was important for Him to know those His Father wanted in this inner circle of His followers.

Besides being present during His public ministry, they spent time alone with Jesus as He instructed them in the ways of God and built their faith. With the exception of Judas who betrayed Him, they would be present at the crucifixion and would see Him in His risen body.

In the accounts of the gospel we are privileged to read what Jesus spoke into the lives of these men. We are given insight into their struggles as well as their triumphs, their failures as well as their successes. We can see the love and patience Jesus exercised in turning these men into the followers He wanted them to become.

Women as well as men were numbered among Jesus' greater number of disciples. A group of women followed Jesus from place to place, caring for His needs (see Mk 15:41). Some of these women followed Him to Jerusalem and were present at the crucifixion.

When giving the disciples the great commission He had for the church, Jesus told them:

> *All authority in heaven and earth has been given to me.*
> *Therefore go and make disciples of all nations, baptising them*
> *in the name of the Father and of the Son and of the Holy Spirit,*
> *teaching them to obey everything I have commanded you.*
> *And surely I am with you always, to the very end of the age.*
> *(Matt 28:18-20)*

These first disciples were themselves to make disciples, teaching them "to obey everything I have commanded you". Jesus was expecting the same obedience from subsequent disciples as He did from these first followers of His. We need to know what He taught them about being disciples if we are to be true followers, therefore. It is not for us to set our standards of discipleship but to fulfil the expectations of Jesus!

Sometimes people want to make a distinction between believers who are saved and disciples who follow Jesus. It is clear from His teaching that every believer in Jesus is to be a disciple. To live as a follower is to live the life of one who is saved. To be saved, a person has to believe that Jesus Christ is the Son of God, that He is the Lord, as well as the Saviour who died on the cross to make it possible for a believer's sins to be forgiven. The believer or disciple is a follower of God's Son, acknowledging that He is the Lord of his or her life.

During His time on earth, many rejected Jesus as divine. *"Yet to all who received him, to those who believed in his name, he gave the right to become children of God ... born of God." (Jn 1:12, 13)* By faith in Jesus as God's Son, the disciple is a child of God, and so a co-heir with Christ:

> *Now if we are children, then we are heirs — heirs of God*
> *and co-heirs with Christ, if indeed we share in his sufferings*
> *in order that we may also share in his glory. (Rom 8:17)*

The disciple is born again and so belongs to the Kingdom of God. Through all Jesus has done for him on the cross, he or she has been saved from eternal punishment. The disciple is forgiven, accepted and is no longer under judgment or condemnation. Jesus said:

> *I tell you the truth, whoever hears my word and believes*
> *him who sent me has eternal life and will not be condemned;*
> *he has crossed over from death to life. (Jn 5:24)*

Prayer: Thank you, Lord Jesus, for calling me to be a disciple. I want to follow you by living according to your Word.

2

GOD'S WONDERFUL PROVISION

The disciple is a child of God, a co-heir with Christ because he or she has been born again, belongs to His Kingdom and has eternal life. He has been forgiven and accepted by God and actually lives in Christ:

*And you also were included in Christ when you heard
the word of truth, the gospel of your salvation. Having believed,
you were marked in him with a seal, the promised Holy Spirit,
who is a deposit guaranteeing our inheritance until the
redemption of those who are God's possession –
to the praise of his glory. (Eph 1:13-14)*

The fact that the disciple has received the Holy Spirit is the very evidence of his acceptance by God and his incorporation into Christ. He or she therefore shares in the inheritance of all who are in Christ. The disciple is blessed *"in the heavenly realms with every spiritual blessing in Christ." (Eph 1:3)*

*For in him you have been enriched in every way – in all your
speaking and in all your knowledge. (1 Cor 1:5)*

Paul continues by saying:

"Therefore you do not lack any spiritual gift." (v7)

Not only is the disciple "in Christ", but Christ lives in him by virtue of the fact that the Holy Spirit lives in him. **The disciple lives in God and God in him; he lives in Christ and Christ in him. He lives in the Spirit and the Spirit in him.**

We know that we live in him and he in us, because he has given us of his Spirit. (1 Jn 4:13)

To understand what Jesus requires of disciples, it is important to know what He has given to those He has called. Those who follow Christ now have an advantage over the disciples during the time Jesus was on earth with them. For at that point they had not died with Christ and been raised to a new life with Him. Neither was the Holy Spirit living in them, although He was working with them.

During the period of the Acts of the Apostles, we see a marked contrast in their lives. The diffident, proud men who often failed to grasp the meaning of what Jesus taught them, who frequently failed and who deserted Him when arrested, became mighty men of God, bold in their preaching, workers of great miracles, who were heedless of the cost of following Christ.

What Jesus taught them could be expressed in their lives once they had received the Holy Spirit. From the very beginning of our discipleship we have the advantage of having received the Holy Spirit, who indwells us and enables us to do whatever Jesus asks of us. This means that whatever Jesus asks of disciples is already made possible for us through the presence and power of His Spirit, who lives in us. **We are already empowered to be the disciples He wants us to be.**

WE ARE ALREADY EMPOWERED TO BE THE DISCIPLES HE WANTS US TO BE.

Paul was not one of the original twelve, yet became probably the most significant figure in the church in New Testament times. He summed up his personal testimony by saying:

> *I have been crucified with Christ and I no longer live, but Christ lives in me. The life I live in the body, I live by faith in the Son of God who loved me and gave himself for me. I do not set aside the grace of God, for if righteousness could be gained through the law, Christ died for nothing! (Gal 2:20-21)*

Within these two verses are a number of truths vital for every disciple to appreciate.

- **When Jesus went to the cross, He took not only your sin, but you, the sinner.** Your old life apart from Him died so that you could be born again and become a new creation in Christ. "For you died, and your life is now hidden with Christ in God." (Col 3:3)

- **The person you were no longer lives!** The old has gone and the new has come. You have a new identity in Christ. So you do not have to look back to your former life. He has separated you from your past, and has freed you to live the new life as His disciple.

- **Christ lives in you by the power of His Spirit.** All the riches and resources of His life are yours. As a disciple, then, Christ wants to live out His life in and through you. **It is not a matter of what you can do for Him, but of Him expressing His life through you.** For this He needs your willing co-operation.

IT IS NOT A MATTER OF WHAT YOU CAN DO FOR HIM, BUT OF HIM EXPRESSING HIS LIFE THROUGH YOU.

- **Jesus is to express His life through your body.** So your body is to be a living sacrifice for Him. A true disciple will not give his heart to the Lord and then live for himself by doing what he likes with his body! "You are not your own; you were bought at a price. Therefore honour God with your body." (1 Cor 6:19 - 20)

- **The disciple lives by faith in Jesus.** He or she is a person of faith. This is the principle by which the disciple lives daily, by putting his or her trust in Jesus. "Without faith it is impossible to please God." (Heb 11:6) The disciple wants to please Him and chooses, therefore, to live by faith.

- **Jesus has demonstrated His love for every disciple by giving His life for him or her.** This is the ultimate expression of love. Note that Paul used the word 'loved', rather than 'loves'. The love of Jesus is not dependent on how He feels about you today! His love is always perfect and complete because He has already shown His love for you by giving His life for you on the cross and then coming to live in you by His Spirit. This means that the disciple never needs to question God's love for him, no matter how difficult the circumstances he may find himself in at times. It is only the devil who suggests: "If God really loves you, why has He allowed this to happen to you?" The disciple knows better. He is secure in the knowledge that Christ has already made the ultimate sacrifice of love for him, and now he lives in the One who is love.

- **The disciple lives by grace.** Grace is the free, unmerited favour of God. It is by His grace that the disciple is saved, forgiven, accepted, has received the gift of God's Kingdom and the fullness of His eternal life. It is by God's grace that he lives in Christ and Christ in him through the power of the Holy Spirit. It is by grace that he has been given every spiritual blessing in Christ and has been enriched in every way:

For you know the grace of our Lord Jesus Christ, that though he was rich, yet for your sakes he became poor, so that you through his poverty might become rich. (2 Cor 8:9)

The disciple has already received so much by grace that he can be confident that God will continue to give him all he needs to live as a faithful disciple. **He has become a disciple by grace, and will live as a disciple by grace.**

- **The disciple has been made righteous,** brought into a right relationship with God by the cleansing away of his sins through the blood of Jesus. Such results cannot be obtained by legalistic religious practices; only by faith in the work of God's grace – all that has been done for the disciple by Jesus.

Having been given such a wonderful relationship at the beginning of his Christian experience, the disciple is not to put aside the grace of God by imagining he can be a true disciple by trying to follow Jesus in his own strength and ability. He will still need to trust daily in the grace of God to enable him to be what Jesus wants him to be, and do what He wants him to do.

> *Therefore, since we have been made right in God's sight through faith, we have peace with God because of what Jesus Christ our Lord has done for us. Because of our faith, Christ has now brought us into this place of highest privilege where we now stand. (Rom 5:1-2 NLT)*

That "place of highest privilege" is the grace of God. **You have become a disciple by grace, and can live as a disciple by grace.**

As we look at the teaching Jesus gave His disciples, you need to remember that this can only be outworked in your life by depending on His grace operating in you by the Holy Spirit. However, you are not a puppet that God forces to do His will. In order for His purpose for your life to be fulfilled, He needs your willing co-operation.

Prayer: Thank you, Lord Jesus, that through your grace I have been crucified with you. My former life has gone and I am now a new creation, called to live by faith in you.

3

THE LIFE OF A DISCIPLE

The great commission is to make disciples, and *"teach them to obey everything I have commanded you."* Jesus expected disciples to live His general teaching as well as to obey any specific commands He gave them as a group.

The Sermon on the Mount is generally regarded as either a typical sermon preached by Jesus, or a collection of sayings common to His teaching. The Sermon is addressed to disciples, before the twelve were appointed. *"His disciples came to him, and he began to teach them." (Matt 5:1-2)*

Certainly the content of the Sermon could only be lived out by followers of Jesus; it speaks of a life that now can only be lived in the power of the Holy Spirit.

Space does not permit us to look at the whole Sermon in detail *(read Matthew chapters 5-7)*. Jesus contrasts the life of those who follow His teaching with those who lived according to religious law and tradition. It is clear that the standards of the new are far higher than the old. Teachers of the law were concerned with outward conformity to religious and traditional practices; Jesus aimed at the heart. **A right heart will lead to right actions, of an altogether higher standard than was possible under the law.**

A RIGHT HEART WILL LEAD TO RIGHT ACTIONS...

The Sermon begins with the "Beatitudes", each beginning with the word "Blessed". This is typical of Jesus, to begin by showing that God's purpose is to bless. He builds people up and encourages them, before speaking whatever correction may need to be spoken into their lives.

To be blessed is to be made happy or fulfilled. And this is what God wants for His children. They are to find their true fulfilment in being the disciples He wants them to be.

The "blessed" are those who are humble, who long to live righteous lives. They have pure hearts. They are merciful to others and spread the gospel of peace – with God and with others. They are even blessed by being persecuted for living as Jesus' followers; their heavenly reward will be great.

The promises Jesus gives to those blessed ones are wonderful. The Kingdom of heaven is theirs and *"they will inherit the earth"*. They are filled with God's life, receive His mercy and forgiveness; they will see God and will then become perfectly like Him! Meanwhile, they are to live as His witnesses here on earth, both as individual believers and corporately. Jesus describes them as *"the salt of the earth" (Matt 5:13)* and *"the light of the world" (v14)*. Clearly, disciples are to impact the society in which they live.

The law condemned murder. Jesus says that anyone angry with his brother is in danger of judgment. The law forbade adultery; Jesus said: *"Anyone who looks at a woman lustfully has already committed adultery with her in his heart" (v28).* The standards of the Kingdom of God are higher than the Law! This is clear in what He says about divorce and the need to exercise forgiveness instead of having attitudes of retribution and vengeance.

Disciples give to the needy. They are praying people, they fast and they live for the cause of His Kingdom, using their resources for this purpose. They live by faith, knowing that if they seek first the Kingdom of God and His righteousness, He will provide for their every need. So they do not need to worry about the provision for the necessities of life.

Jesus warns the disciples not to judge; if they do they will place themselves under the same judgment with which they judge others.

Jesus encourages the disciples to ask in prayer, promising that *"everyone who asks receives" (Matt 7:8). How much more will your Father in heaven give good gifts to those who ask him! (7:11)*

He is concerned about the disciple's relationship with God and with others. As the apostle John was to make clear, you cannot love God who you do not see unless you love your brother who you can see - a principle he clearly learned from Jesus. John also learned from Jesus that genuine love for God is expressed in obedience. Jesus said:

> *Not everyone who says to me, 'Lord, Lord', will enter the Kingdom of heaven, but only he who does the will of my Father who is in heaven." (Matt 7:21)*

A religion of words is not enough. A disciple does not only desire to please Jesus; he does His will. He lives the gospel. This is wisdom:

> *Therefore everyone who hears these words of mine and*
> *puts them into practice is like a wise man who built his house*
> *on the rock. (Matt 7:24)*

Because of its secure foundation, that house was able to withstand the battering it received from storms. The foolish man, by contrast, hears the word but does not obey it. His house is built on sand and collapses under the pressure of adverse circumstances.

Prayer: Thank you, Lord Jesus, that you enable me to live by the standards of your Kingdom. I want your Kingdom to come and your will to be done in my life.

4

THE KINGDOM OF GOD

Besides the general teaching given to the crowds or a greater number of disciples, Jesus spoke to the twelve when He took them aside on their own to disciple them. Before ascending to heaven He instructed them to make disciples, who would obey everything He had commanded them. All disciples of Jesus, now as in Bible times, are to obey what He taught these first disciples both publicly and in His private times with them away from the public gaze.

Several of these statements seem radical. This is only because what we see in churches generally today is a level of discipleship far below the standards expected by Jesus. We have seen that essentially a disciple is one to whom the Lord has given the abundance of His life through His grace. However, much is expected of those to whom much is given!

The original twelve not only heard Jesus teach, they observed the way He ministered to the needs of the crowds of people who came to Him. To watch Him at work was one thing; to be expected to do the same things themselves was quite another! No doubt they felt really challenged when Jesus sent them out in ministry.

However, He made sure that they were fully equipped for everything He asked of them:

> *He called his twelve disciples to him and gave them*
> *authority to drive out evil spirits and to heal every disease*
> *and sickness. (Matt 10:1)*

We cannot confine this authority as belonging only to the twelve. When Jesus sent seventy-two disciples out to prepare the way for the places to which He was going, He told them:

> *Heal the sick who are there and tell them, 'The kingdom*
> *of God is near you.' (Luke 10:9)*

These disciples returned to Jesus with joy that even demons had submitted to them in Jesus' name. Jesus told them:

> *I have given you authority to trample on snakes and scorpions and*
> *to overcome all the power of the enemy; nothing will harm you.*
> *However, do not rejoice that the spirits submit to you, but rejoice*
> *that your names are written in heaven. (Luke 10:19-20)*

Jesus then went on to praise His Father that such revelation had been given not to 'the wise and learned', but to 'little children'!

God's children today are given the same authority because they too belong to God's Kingdom. Jesus' teaching and ministry was centred on the Kingdom. He taught the disciples to pray that His Kingdom would come and His will be done on earth as in heaven. The Sermon on the Mount is a description of what it means to live the life of God's heavenly Kingdom here on earth. And these words of commission, to both the twelve and the seventy-two, demonstrate that Jesus was entrusting to them the authority of the Kingdom, the same authority that He Himself exercised over the devil and all his works. **They could exercise the authority of the Kingdom because they belonged to the Kingdom. And the same is true for disciples today!**

Jesus never taught without using parables, and these are stories that teach us about the nature of God's Kingdom and the One who rules over it. They speak of the present reality of the Kingdom and also of the future fulfilment of that Kingdom. Jesus told His disciples:

Do not be afraid, little flock, for your Father has been pleased to give you the kingdom. (Luke 12:32)

The Kingdom comes as a gift to His followers. To receive that gift implies that they will be prepared to devote their lives to living for the cause of the Kingdom of God. Jesus explained to the Pharisees:

The kingdom of God does not come with your careful observation, nor will people say, 'Here it is', or 'There it is', because the kingdom of God is within you. (Luke 17:20-21)

This Kingdom that comes as a gift to the disciples is the rule and reign of God within their hearts and lives. Jesus likened this Kingdom to a seed:

Then Jesus asked, "What is the kingdom of God like? What shall I compare it to? It is like a mustard seed, which a man took and planted in his garden. It grew and became a tree, and the birds of the air perched in its branches. (Luke 13:18-19)

The tree is contained in the seed. It only needs the right conditions to grow: good soil, light and water. Then it can develop into the fruitful plant it has been created to be. The good soil for the life of the Kingdom is the good heart, a heart that loves the Lord. In such a life there can be a harvest:

The seed on good soil stands for those with a noble and good heart, who hear the word, retain it, and by perseverance produce a crop. (Luke 8:15)

That crop is *"a hundred times more than was sown"*. *(v8)*

The light needed by the disciple is the word of God, and the water is the living water of the Holy Spirit. **This enables the disciple to be fruitful and reproduce the life of the Kingdom he or she has been given: a good heart, the word of God and the life and power of the Holy Spirit. He or she is supplied with everything needed to live as a child of the Kingdom.**

Kingdom life within the believer will grow and develop if nurtured in the right way. However, in the parable of the sower, Jesus warns that if the message of the Kingdom falls on a hard heart, it is snatched away by the enemy. The word of the Kingdom that is not nurtured will not survive the pressures of life. Those who begin well will fall away, if they allow the cares of this life to choke the seed.

This gift of the Kingdom is so valuable that Jesus likens it to treasure hidden in a field. *"When a man found it, he hid it again, and then in his joy went and sold all he had and bought that field."* (Matt 13:44)

It is like a pearl of great value that a merchant sold all he had to possess. *(Matt 13:45-46)* Jesus does not mean to imply from these parables that it is possible to buy your way into the Kingdom, but that it is worth more than everything else you have, even the sum total of all you possess.

For disciples to possess this gift of the Kingdom does not satisfy Jesus. He expects to see them living the life of that Kingdom, preparing for the return of Jesus, when He will come again, not as the Suffering Servant, but as the Triumphant King in all His glory! Meanwhile, they are to devote their lives not only to living the life of this Kingdom, but to seeing this Kingdom extended into the hearts and lives of more and more people. Instead of using their money and resources for earthly ends, they are to lay up treasures for themselves in heaven by using their resources for the work of the Kingdom.

The values of the Kingdom are totally at odds with the values held dear by those who belong to this world. When asked by the disciples why He spoke in parables not readily understood by everyone, Jesus explained:

> *The knowledge of the secrets of the kingdom of heaven has been given to you, but not to them. Whoever has will be given more, and he will have an abundance. Whoever does not have, even what he has will be taken from him. (Matt 13:11-12)*

The reality of the Kingdom cannot be understood by those who do not belong to it. The disciples were privileged to receive the revelation of the Kingdom. As the life of that Kingdom grows within them, they will receive blessing upon blessing through

God's grace. They will have all they need in this life and a rich reward in heaven.

Those who reject the offer of God's Kingdom will lose what they have now, and have no eternal inheritance to look forward to! True disciples live this Kingdom life now on earth and know an eternal destiny awaits them in God's glory! However, as Jesus Himself demonstrated:

Even the Son of Man did not come to be served, but to serve, and to give his life as a ransom for many. (Mk 10:45)

When asked who is the greatest in the Kingdom, He took a child and placed him among the disciples. He told them that they had to be like little children to enter the Kingdom of heaven:

Therefore, whoever humbles himself like this child is the greatest in the kingdom of heaven. (Matt 18:4)

We all long for the glory that will come with the return of Jesus. Meanwhile, we are to live as humble servants in God's Kingdom - sons of God who are called to serve! At the judgment the King will divide the sheep from the goats. The sheep are those who have served. Jesus said:

For I was hungry and you gave me something to eat, I was thirsty and you gave me something to drink, I was a stranger and you invited me in, I needed clothes and you clothed me, I was sick and you looked after me, I was in prison and you came to visit me. (Matt 25:35-36)

The sheep are mystified by these words. So Jesus explains to them:

"I tell you the truth, whatever you did for one of the least of these brothers of mine, you did for me." (Matt 25:40)

Because of their servant hearts they had readily reached out to others to help and bless them, not realising that in doing this they had been serving the King of kings.

By contrast, the goats were mystified by their rejection. If only they had realised that Jesus identified with those in need, then they would have served them. Too late! Their opportunity has gone. They chose to live for themselves, rather than for the King and His Kingdom.

This shows how practical it is to live the life of the Kingdom here on earth. The values of the Kingdom of God are so different from those of the world. In the world you are successful to have others serve you. In the Kingdom of God you are great if you serve others! In the world people seek status, position and acclaim from others. In God's Kingdom it is the humble that He chooses to exalt. In fact, He resists the proud and pulls them down!

In the world you are expected to get as much as you can for yourself. If you give you are taught that you will be worse off. Quite the opposite is true of those who belong to God's Kingdom:

Give, and it will be given to you. A good measure, pressed down, shaken together and running over, will be poured into your lap. For with the measure you use, it will be measured to you. (Luke 6:38)

Again, this is a matter of the heart. Whatever is in the heart of a person will be expressed in what he says and does. The disciple who produces the good fruit of God's Kingdom does so because his heart is right towards God and he therefore has the right priorities. He wants to glorify the Lord by fulfilling His plan and purpose for his life. So he seeks first the Kingdom of God and His righteousness. Jesus said:

> *No good tree bears bad fruit, nor does a bad tree bear good fruit.*
> *Each tree is recognised by its own fruit. People do not pick*
> *figs from thornbushes, or grapes from briers. The good man brings*
> *good things out of the good stored up in his heart, and the evil man*
> *brings evil things out of the evil stored up in his heart. For out of the*
> *overflow of the heart his mouth speaks. (Luke 6:43-45)*

Prayer: Thank you, Lord Jesus, that you have made available to me all the riches and resources of your Kingdom. By your love and mercy, I shall be numbered among your sheep.

5

NOT SELF

Jesus' teaching is too practical for comfort, if you love the flesh! To love the flesh is to desire to live for yourself, to please yourself. This is totally the opposite of what Jesus expects of His disciples:

> *Then Jesus said to his disciples, "If anyone would come*
> *after me, he must deny himself and take up his cross and follow me.*
> *For whoever wants to save his life will lose it, but whoever*
> *loses his life for me will find it." (Matt 16:24 - 25)*

To be a disciple of Jesus involves nothing less than *"losing your life"*. No longer living for yourself, but for your Lord and Master. No longer living to fulfil your own fleshly desires and ambitions, but longing to fulfil His desires for you. In fact, Paul even said that those with selfish ambition *"will not inherit the kingdom of God."* *(Gal 5:21)*

Even Jesus had a soul or self life during His humanity. But He kept Himself submitted to the will of His Father at all times. He explained: *"For I have come down from heaven not to do my will but to do the will of him who sent me." (Jn 6:38)*

And when there was a danger of His will coming into conflict with that of His Father, He prayed: *"Yet not what I will, but what you will." (Mk 14:36)*

So for the disciple, called to follow Jesus, there has to be the willingness to deny his own will in order to serve the interests of His Lord and His Kingdom. To be willing to serve Him by serving others, even if that is sometimes costly and inconvenient.

Jesus does not hide the fact that it will be costly to be His disciple, and will involve a complete re-ordering of a person's priorities:

> *The man who loves his life will lose it, while the man who hates his life in this world will keep it for eternal life. Whoever serves me must follow me; and where I am, my servant also will be. My Father will honour the one who serves me. (Jn 12:25-26)*

There are a number of important truths to note from this scripture:

- Jesus is talking about everyone, not some elite.

- To love your life, to live for yourself, means you will lose your life.

- To keep himself for eternal life, a man will have to hate his life in this world. In the New Testament the word translated "hate" does not mean to act viciously or vindictively. It is simply an absence of love. To hate your life in this world is not to love your life in this world. In other words, it is not to love worldliness, but to see yourself as a citizen of God's heavenly Kingdom, called to live by the life and values of that Kingdom in the midst of a world where the vast majority live to please themselves!

- Whoever serves Jesus, who is His disciple, must follow Him. This is not an option; it is a necessity! Either you live as a disciple or you don't!

- To follow Jesus is to be where He is, allowing Him to lead you wherever He wants you to go, to do what He wants you to do, and be what He wants you to be!

As with His own life, so with the disciple; Jesus likens his life to that of a seed that has to fall into the ground and die. Otherwise it cannot grow, develop and be fruitful. The life of a disciple remains only a single seed until such time as he or she comes to the realisation that it is necessary to die to self in order to follow Jesus.

He died to Himself in order to be obedient to the Father, and we cannot follow Him, unless we follow this example, to be where He is! If this seems radical, Jesus has more to say on the subject:

Anyone who loves his father or mother more than me is not worthy of me; anyone who loves his son or daughter more than me is not worthy of me; and anyone who does not take his cross and follow me is not worthy of me. (Matt 10:37-38)

It is clear that as our Lord, Jesus needs to be on the throne of our lives. His authority and place are to have no rivals! Even from those who are closest to us!

Those who have yielded their lives to Jesus in such a way, so they can live as His disciples, will testify that this enriches the lives of their loved ones. You cannot give to God without Him giving immeasurably more back to you. Jesus was even more outspoken on another occasion.

> *Large crowds were travelling with Jesus, and turning to them*
> *he said: "If anyone comes to me and does not hate his father*
> *and mother, his wife and children, his brothers and sisters - yes,*
> *even his own life - he cannot be my disciple. And anyone who does*
> *not carry his cross and follow me cannot be my disciple."*
> *(Luke 14:25-27)*

How are we to understand such words? Obviously Jesus does not mean disciples are to feel venomous hatred towards their loved ones. This would conflict with all He teaches about loving one another.

Jesus uses the word "hate" when making comparisons, or speaking of the personal preferences people choose to have. For example, He says it is impossible to serve two masters; for you will love one and hate the other. You are not to love your life in preference to Christ, therefore. Neither are you to prefer mother, father, wife, children, brothers or sisters to Christ. Jesus is to be your Number One at all times.

Why does Jesus put this so strongly? If you are to be His disciple there can be no compromise as to who is reigning in your life. You are to hate the very idea of placing yourself before Jesus. What a terrible thought! Daring to place yourself before the Lord of lords and King of kings.

Likewise, you are to hate the idea of placing anyone else before

Jesus, no matter how much you love them or how precious they are to you. Your love for Jesus is to be supreme, greater than your love for anyone else. Otherwise you cannot be His disciple.

The commission for the church is to make disciples, those who love Jesus in such a way, placing Him first at all times. This is the cost that needs to be counted by anyone who wants to be a disciple.

You can see what a disservice it has been to the cause of God's Kingdom for some Christians to give people the impression that you only have to make a token response to the gospel at a meeting to be saved. This is far from the truth that Jesus teaches.

We are saved by grace, by His activity alone, so that we can live as disciples. The cause of God's Kingdom is hindered, not helped, by casually-minded, disobedient believers who give the impression that God is satisfied by coming to live in the heart – even if the person continues to live a disobedient, even rebellious, life.

When He speaks about the cost of being a disciple, Jesus concludes:

> *In the same way, any of you who does not give up everything*
> *he has cannot be my disciple (Luke 14:33)*

This needs no explanation; it is clear what Jesus is saying! Some are tempted to think that there are two categories of people: Christians who believe in Jesus and are therefore saved; and those who have forsaken everything to be His disciples.

That sounds convenient. **However, the commission is to make**

ALL CHRISTIANS, ALL BELIEVERS IN JESUS CHRIST, ARE CALLED TO BE DISCIPLES AND TO OBEY EVERYTHING JESUS COMMANDED THOSE FIRST DISCIPLES.

disciples, not converts. And all Christians, all believers in Jesus Christ, are called to be disciples and to obey everything Jesus commanded those first disciples.

This truth will cause many to reassess what it means to be a Christian in practice as well as name. What today would be called radical discipleship is, in the New Testament, normal Christian life!

It is not a question of making comparisons but of asking the question as to whether Jesus has reduced His expectations of disciples since His time on earth. We can reject that idea because we know His words endure forever! And notice that these last quotations were addressed to the large crowds that followed Jesus. They were not words addressed to an elite minority. The apostle Paul said:

I consider everything a loss compared to the surpassing greatness of knowing Christ Jesus my Lord, for whose sake I have lost all things. I consider them rubbish, that I may gain Christ and be found in him. (Phil 3:8-9)

As a disciple of Jesus, Paul took His words seriously: *"Whoever loses his life for me will find it." (Matt 16:25)*

Jesus also made clear to those who believed in Him as true disciples, obeyed His words. They did not try to avoid what He said, or interpret His words in ways that suited the level of commitment by which they had chosen to live. No, disciples can only follow Jesus on His terms, not their own!

If you hold to my teaching, you are really my disciples.
Then you will know the truth, and the truth
will set you free. (Jn 8:31-32)

Jesus is saying that the very evidence that proves a person is a true disciple is that he or she both believes and therefore lives according to His word. It is for this reason that every disciple is given the precious gift of God's Holy Spirit. He or she is not trying to fulfil God's word and follow Jesus in his or her own human strength and ability, but through the anointing of the Holy Spirit.

Prayer: Thank you, Lord Jesus, that you have called me to deny myself, take up my cross and follow you. May I not place myself or others before you, but allow you to be Lord in every part of my life.

6

LOVE FOR JESUS

Of course, a person can only follow the Lord with such surrender to Him if he or she has a genuine love for Him. *If you love me, you will obey what I command. (Jn 14:15)* Obedience comes out of this love relationship with Jesus Christ.

> *"Whoever has my commands and obeys them, he is the one who loves me. He who loves me will be loved by my Father, and I too will love him and show myself to him." (Jn 14:21)*

The benefits that come from knowing Jesus are great. Obedience to Him enables the disciple to remain in His love and for his or her joy to be full. (see Jn 15:9-11) **It is easy to say you love Jesus, but such a statement is only true if you obey Him!** The apostle John, who was present when Jesus spoke these words, wrote about fifty years later: *"Dear children, let us not love with words or tongue but with actions and in truth." (1 Jn 3:18)*

Many Christians deceive themselves by saying they are really committed to the Lord. What does this mean? This is not a biblical way of thinking. Neither Jesus nor the New Testament writers talk of commitment. No, they speak of obedience, not commitment.

However, you do not hear people say: "I am an obedient Christian". Yet this is what Jesus wants every disciple to be able to say!

This does not mean that He waits for us to reach a high state of spirituality before He accepts us as disciples. No, He accepts us at the very beginning of our Christian walk, but then initiates the process of discipleship, leading each follower to *"become mature, attaining to the whole measure of the fullness of Christ." (Eph 4:13)* You become spiritually mature by obeying God's word, not by disobedience to Jesus! It is only by loving obedience that we can follow Christ. The disobedient will not follow. The rebellious, independently-minded will even oppose what He wants.

Because of the disciple's love for Jesus, he will want to do what pleases Him. And this will draw the disciple into a relationship and walk with Jesus that will inspire great faith and confidence in him:

> *Dear friends, if our hearts do not condemn us, we have confidence before God and receive from him anything we ask, because we obey his commands and do what pleases him. (1 Jn 3:21-22)*

And what are these commands that disciples have to obey? In the next verse John explains: *And this is his command: to believe in the name of his Son, Jesus Christ, and to love one another as he commanded us. (1 Jn 3:23)*

Faith working through love, the very lifestyle that Paul describes as *"the only thing that counts". (Gal 5:6)*

Prayer: Thank you, Lord Jesus, for giving me the love that will enable me to obey you in all things.

7

FAITH AND LOVE TOGETHER

Both John and Paul reflected Jesus' dislike, contempt even, for "super-spirituality" – those who have the right language, but not the right lifestyle. Those who are all talk, but who do little or nothing to love, serve and bless others. "The kingdom of God is not a matter of talk but of power", says Paul (1 Cor 4:20) Super-spiritual people have plenty of talk but little power. They are often highly critical, displaying attitudes similar to those of the Pharisees in Jesus' time.

True spirituality is expressed in action! Otherwise the believer only has "dead faith". *Faith by itself, if it is not accompanied by action, is dead. (James 2:17)*

It is not a question of faith or love; but faith and love, faith in love, faith working through love. And that love is only real if expressed in obedience. So Paul states his task clearly:

> *Through him and for his name's sake, we received grace and apostleship to call people from among all the Gentiles to the obedience that comes from faith. (Rom 1:5)*

So true faith leads to obedient action. True love also is expressed in obedient action! To those who love Jesus, such obedience is not a burden:

This is love for God: to obey his commands. And his commands are not burdensome. (1 Jn 5:3)

Commands are only a burden when you do not want to obey them! Your love for Jesus transcends the cost of obedience.

OBEDIENCE TO GOD'S WORD IS THE ONLY WAY TO MEASURE TRUE COMMITMENT, FAITH OR LOVE.

If a child is sick, his loving parent will nurse him, care for him, sit with him all night if necessary. Love for the child is greater than the cost of caring for him. The parent does not say it is too costly to love, and leave the child to fend for himself!

John goes on to say that this obedience is the outworking of faith that enables us to overcome the world. Having the right words of faith will not always enable you to see victory. But when those words are expressed in an obedient life of faith and love, then powerful things are going to result.

Obedience to God's Word is the only way to measure true commitment, faith or love.

Many speak of themselves as committed Christians simply because they have given their hearts to the Lord. This is not New Testament thinking. What good is a heart without a body? A heart cannot walk down the road to serve or love people.

Obedience and faith can only be expressed by what the body says and does. Paul writes:

> *Do you not know that your body is a temple of the*
> *Holy Spirit, who is in you, whom you have received from God?*
> *You are not your own; you were bought at a price.*
> *Therefore honour God with your body. (1 Cor 6:19-20)*

Elsewhere Paul says that believers are to offer their bodies *"in slavery to righteousness leading to holiness." (Rom 6:19)* He also writes:

> *Therefore I urge you, brothers, in view of God's mercy, to offer*
> *your bodies as living sacrifices, holy and pleasing to God - this is*
> *your spiritual act of worship. (Rom 12:1)*

The message is unmistakable. The disciple belongs to the Lord in spirit, soul and body – all that he is and all that he has. Jesus purchased him for God with His own blood. He no longer belongs to himself, and so is not to live for himself! As a disciple he denies himself, takes up his cross and follows Jesus.

THE DISCIPLE BELONGS TO THE LORD IN SPIRIT, SOUL AND BODY ...

He recognises he is called to a life of love and faith. Only in this way can he be a true disciple of Jesus, a true follower!

Prayer: Thank you, Lord Jesus, that faith and love will work together in my life. I give you my body as a temple of your Holy Spirit to be used for your glory.

8

LIVING TO SERVE

What does it mean in practice to live a life of faith working through love? Jesus encouraged the disciples to trust Him in all things at all times. And He encouraged them to obey His words of command, the obedience that would be the evidence and outworking of their love for Him. The focus for Jesus was always the outworking of the Father's will and the fruit that was to be produced as a result, for His glory. He encouraged His disciples to have the same focus.

All disciples are called to love and serve others; in this way they express their love for Jesus and truly serve Him. When Jesus spoke of the separation of the sheep and goats, it is clear that the goats failed to love and serve those in need. So Jesus explains:

'I tell you the truth, whatever you did not do for one of the least of these, you did not do for me'. Then they will go away to eternal punishment, but the righteous to eternal life. (Matt 25:45)

It is not for us to judge anyone; all judgment has been entrusted to the Son. It is clear that all true disciples will be included among the sheep. It is equally clear, therefore, that Jesus expects true disciples to express their love for Him by serving others in practical ways. There is no room for super-spirituality or unreality here. Were the goats guilty of such attitudes?

Faith will lead to the works of faith, and God will give to every disciple the necessary grace to perform those works in His name. Love will lead to the practical works of love. The apostle John is as outspoken as Jesus:

> *We know that we have come to know him if we obey*
> *his commands. The man who says, "I know him", but does not*
> *do what he commands is a liar, and the truth is not in him.*
> *But if anyone obeys his word, God's love is truly made*
> *complete in him. (1 Jn 2:3-5)*

John's message is clear: **To know Jesus is to love Jesus; to love Jesus is to obey Jesus; to obey Jesus is to love others! This is true discipleship, what it means to live as a follower of Jesus Christ.** *"Whoever loves his brother lives in the light, and there is nothing in him to make him stumble." (1 Jn 2:10) "The man who does the will of God lives forever." (1 Jn 2:17)*

It is all so practical! Because Jesus laid His life down for us, we ought to lay down our lives for others, living to serve them rather than to please ourselves. This is in stark contrast to the values of modern western society! We are to love with actions and in truth, not only with words and sentiment! (see 1 Jn 3:16-18)

> *Everyone who loves has been born of God and knows God.*
> *(1 Jn 4:7)*

The implications are clear: if **a person does not live to serve others, he or she does not truly know Jesus and cannot be a disciple of His!** Yet every disciple knows that he or she can only love because Jesus has first loved us. The obedience of loving service towards others is a response to the great love that Jesus has expressed by giving His life for us.

THE LORD WANTS YOU TO GROW IN GREATNESS ...

Jesus did not come to lord it over people, but to express the love in God's heart by serving people. His heart of compassion drew people to Him so their needs could be met:

Come to me, all you who are weary and burdened, and I will give you rest. Take my yoke upon you and learn from me, for I am gentle and humble in heart, and you will find rest for your souls. (Matt 11:28-29)

This is the Son of Man, full of authority and power, yet with a gentle, humble servant heart. No wonder He said:

"Whoever wants to become great among you must be your servant, and whoever wants to be first must be your slave – just as the Son of Man did not come to be served, but to serve, and to give his life as a ransom for many."
(Matt 20:26-28)

The Lord wants you to grow in greatness, to be great in His Kingdom. He says the way for this to happen is for you to be a servant, a sheep, a true disciple. This is not a doctrine of works in order to be saved. It is listening to what Jesus says about what it means to live as one who is saved. Salvation will be expressed in many practical ways of loving service.

The first responsibility of the five-fold ministry is *"to prepare God's people for works of service." (Eph 4:12)* In serving others, we serve the Lord. We cannot serve Him without serving others:

> *Serve wholeheartedly, as if you were serving the Lord,*
> *not men, because you know the Lord will reward everyone for*
> *whatever good he does. (Eph 6:7-8)*

Jesus says that whoever practices and teaches His commands will be called great in the Kingdom of heaven. (see Matt 5:19) He does not say practice or teach, but practice and teach! He wants disciples to be great in His Kingdom because they practice His commandments of love and teach others to do likewise.

Prayer: Thank you, Lord Jesus, for the wonderful privilege of serving you and others. Work in me the servant heart I need.

9

A LOVING HEART

Obviously, Jesus is not talking about legalistic obedience. The disciple is to have a heart of love. His actions, decisions and relationships are motivated by love for God and for people. **A disciple with a loving heart will love the Lord. He will also love his brothers and sisters in Christ. He will love his neighbour, the lost, poor, the needy and desperate. He will love because of the loving nature of his heart. Even his faith will be expressed in love!**

Love is patient, love is kind. It does not envy, it does not boast, it is not proud. It is not rude, it is not self-seeking, it is not easily angered, it keeps no record of wrongs. Love does not delight in evil but rejoices with the truth. It always protects, always trusts, always hopes, always perseveres. Love never fails. (1 Cor 13:4-8)

Go through this passage slowly, phrase by phrase, and you will see how very practical this love is. Absolutely no room for impractical super-spirituality! This is the love that God's Holy Spirit wants to work in every disciple of Jesus.

What is in the heart will determine the way a person lives and speaks! The disciple with a loving heart will live a life of loving service for others. Those with selfish ambition have no inheritance in the Kingdom.

In His ministry, Jesus exposed the hypocrisy in the hearts of the Pharisees and other religious legalists. There is no point in appearing righteous on the outside if the heart is full of greed and self-indulgence.

By contrast, the one with a right heart will live a life of true righteousness. He will reflect something of the Lord's heart, full of mercy, grace and love.

The true disciple is a loving and forgiving person. A man or woman of faith certainly; for without faith it is impossible to please God.

The true disciple is a praying person, knowing he or she is called to fulfil God's plan and purpose for his or her life.

The true disciple wants to be led by the Holy Spirit, and becomes increasingly confident of being able to hear the voice of God!

The true disciple desires to obey the Lord by obeying His commands, especially His command to love others. He is willing to *"lay down his life for his friends"*: to live for others rather than himself.

The true disciple is motivated, not by selfish ambition, but by a desire to please the Lord.

The true disciple wants to bear much fruit for the Father's glory.

The true disciple learns to persevere and does not easily give up when faced with opposition or persecution. The true disciple is determined to remain faithful to the end!

THE TRUE DISCIPLE IS DETERMINED TO REMAIN FAITHFUL TO THE END!

The true disciple learns to live in the supernatural power of God, made available through the authority given him by Jesus. By exercising this authority and using this power, he is able to do the same things as Jesus, and even greater things still. For now the Spirit has been poured out freely in a way that had not yet happened during Jesus' earthly ministry.

The true disciple has been given the knowledge of the secrets of God's Kingdom. By God's grace, he is able to live the life of the Kingdom in the power of the Holy Spirit.

The true disciple knows his own weakness and vulnerability, the need to depend completely on Jesus. He is well aware of the mercy and grace that need to be extended to him day by day because, all too frequently, he fails to measure up to the standards that will please the Lord. What God does accomplish through him is completely the work of His grace, and so all the glory goes to Him!

The true disciple knows he is not judged and condemned by the Lord when he fails. God wants to lead him in His triumphant procession. However, because of his love for his Lord and Master, the disciple does not want to fail Him. He longs to fulfil the destiny for which he was called and chosen to be a disciple!

The true disciple wants to become more and more like Jesus, being transformed into His likeness with ever-increasing glory.

And we, who with unveiled faces all reflect the Lord's glory, are being transformed into his likeness with ever-increasing glory, which comes from the Lord, who is the Spirit. (2 Cor 3:18)

The disciple is encouraged by the fact that Jesus restored Peter when he denied Him, and all the disciples when they deserted Him at the time of His arrest. Frequently He forgave their sins and unbelief. Continually He encouraged them to believe that they could do whatever He could do, if their trust was in Him.

HE WILL SHOW YOU INFINITE PATIENCE AND KINDNESS, BUT NEVER WILL HE LOSE SIGHT OF THE PURPOSE HE HAS FOR YOU ...

So to be a disciple is to belong to Jesus' school! He will teach you, train you, equip you. He will correct you and discipline you in love. He will purify your heart and motivate you for His Kingdom purposes. He will show you infinite patience and kindness, but never will He lose sight of the purpose He has for you in calling you to be His disciple.

He knew what He was getting when He called you. You have never surprised Him! Lovingly He will continue to lead you in the way in which He wants you to walk, so you will accomplish the part He has for you in His purposes that He is working out in the nations. He sees you as having a significant part to play, or He would not have called you!

However, He makes clear that your obedience to His will needs to be wholehearted, without any compromise, because you are ready to deny yourself, seek first His Kingdom and righteousness, and follow Him! In this He greatly encourages you.

And He sees you as belonging to His family:

> *"Who is my mother, and who are my brothers?"*
> *Pointing to his disciples, he said, "Here are my mother and my*
> *brothers. For whoever does the will of my Father in heaven is my*
> *brother and sister and mother." (Matt 12:48-50)*

Jesus was a man of prayer. It was imperative He drew aside to spend time praying to His Father. He constantly drew the twelve disciples aside, so that He could teach and impart to them whatever they needed in order for them to fulfil His call to be disciples.

It is imperative, in the same way, that you allow Jesus to take you aside, to speak to you through the Word, to teach and train you, to build and encourage your faith. It is vitally necessary for you to develop your relationship with Him in prayer and for you to become familiar with the voice of His Spirit.

In other words, any true disciple will be a man or woman of the Spirit, and therefore of prayer. The disciple will not neglect his spiritual life. Even though he is called to a life of active faith and love, he recognises his need to be sensitive to God's voice. He needs to believe what the Spirit is telling him to believe, and to do what the Spirit leads him to do.

Although he deserves nothing and lives dependent on the grace of God, the disciple wants to hear his Master say:

> *Well done, good and faithful servant! You have been faithful with*
> *a few things; I will put you in charge of many things. Come and*
> *share your master's happiness! (Matt 25:23)*

Prayer: Thank you, Lord Jesus, that as your disciple you will continue to teach, train and equip me in every way to do your will. I will accept your loving correction and discipline when needed. May I also seek first your Kingdom and your Righteousness. Amen.

The True Series will comprise the following titles:

TRUE ANOINTING
TRUE APOSTLES
TRUE CHURCH
TRUE DELIVERANCE
TRUE DEVOTION
TRUE DISCIPLES
TRUE FAITH
TRUE FREEDOM
TRUE GRACE
TRUE HEALING
TRUE HOLINESS
TRUE JUDGMENT
TRUE KINGDOM
TRUE LIFE
TRUE LORD
TRUE LOVE
TRUE MISSION
TRUE PRAYER
TRUE SALVATION
TRUE WISDOM
TRUE WORSHIP

All these books by Colin Urquhart and a catalogue of other titles and teaching materials can be obtained from:

Kingdom Faith Resources, Roffey Place, Old Crawley Road
Faygate, Horsham, West Sussex RH12 4RU.
Telephone 01293 854 600 email: resources@kingdomfaith.com